The Wonders of Nature Sketchbook

Written by Colleen Monroe • Illustrated by Michael Glenn Monroe

Storytime Press
427 W. Main St.
Brighton, MI 48116
www.storytimepress.com

Book design by Graphikitchen LLC

Printed and bound in the USA

10 9 8 7 6 5

Library of Congress Cataloging-in-Publication Data
Monroe, Colleen.
    The wonders of nature sketchbook / written by Colleen Monroe ; illustrated by Michael Glenn Monroe.

    p. : ill. ; cm.
    ISBN: 0-9754942-1-X

1. Animals in art--Juvenile literature. 2. Wildlife art--Juvenile literature. 3. Drawing--Technique--Juvenile literature. 4. Animals in art. 5. Drawing--Technique. 6. Animals. I. Monroe, Michael Glenn. II. Title.

NC780 .M66 2005
743.6   2005908448

To our children: Natalie, Matthew and John,
who continue to inspire us on a daily basis.

Colleen Monroe

To all the people that in some way work to save our
natural world for the generations to come.

Michael Monroe

Drawing Tips

Draw very softly so that you will not have to erase harsh dark lines later as you begin to choose the lines that you like best for your drawing.

To start any animal drawing you should first begin to create the general shape of the animal with simple shapes. Use circles, triangles and ovals.

1

Medium oval for head

Small oval for bill

Large oval for body

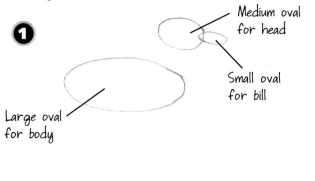

2

Curved line for neck

Add eye

Long, slender triangle for wing

Shorter, broader triangle for tail

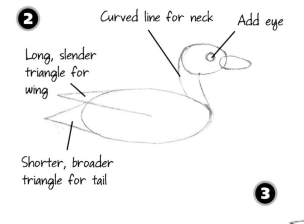

3

Small triangle for inside of tail

Connect bill to head

4

Erase unwanted lines

This is called the "writing position". Most of our drawing will be done with the pencil in this position using the tip of the pencil lead.

This is the "underhand position". This is the position you will use when adding shading to your drawing. Notice how wide the pencil line is in this position.

Learning to Shade

It doesn't matter what shape your subject is, in order to look three dimensional and more realistic you will have to use shading. Shading allows you to add shadows and light areas which are made from the light source...in nature that would be the sun. The areas of your subject that are the farthest from the sun will be shaded the darkest and the areas that are the closest to the sun will remain the lightest. Once you have shaded in your animal you will be ready to add details like feathers or fur.

Sunlight from front of duck

Sunlight from back of duck

Sunlight from above duck

Hummingbirds

The adult Ruby-throat grows to an average length of 3¾ inches from the tip of the beak to the end of the tail. It only weighs as much as a penny.

There are almost 400 different species of hummingbirds throughout the world. The Ruby-throated hummingbird is the most common in the Eastern United States. It's named for the beautiful iridescent red feathers found on the chin of the male.

Hummingbirds beat their wings an average of 50-80 times per second. During their courtship activities, they can beat them almost 250 times per second!

Female hummingbirds often build their nests near water. The inside dimension of the nest is less than 2 inches and usually holds 1-2 eggs that are the size of small jellybeans. The nest is often made out of plant materials and spiderwebs. Sometimes the female will use bits of lichen on the outside of the nest.

1 Hint – draw softly!

Start with a long oval for the body

Draw a small oval for the head

Triangle for tail

2 Draw two lines to start the wings

Add a soft, curved line for the bottom of the beak

3 Draw the top of the beak

Add second triangle for other side of tail

Remember — hummingbirds have long, skinny beaks!

4 Add the eye

Draw the bottom of each wing

5 Draw a short line for the back of the neck

Draw a short line for the throat

6 Erase unwanted lines

Create a place for the hummingbird to live. They love gardens & all types of flowers. Maybe add some other garden creatures.

Birds

There are many unusual and interesting birds. One such bird is the kingfisher. It will wait patiently on a branch that hangs over a body of water. When it sees a fish or frog it will dive head first into the water to catch its prey, sometimes diving to a depth of 2 feet.

Other birds, like the downy woodpecker have unique tools to help find their food. The smallest of all the woodpeckers found in the United States, the downy uses its tiny bill to chisel holes in trees where it finds insects for its meal.

Another unusual bird is the white-breasted nuthatch. Using its strong feet the nuthatch can travel headfirst up and down the tree trunks, sometimes hanging upside down.

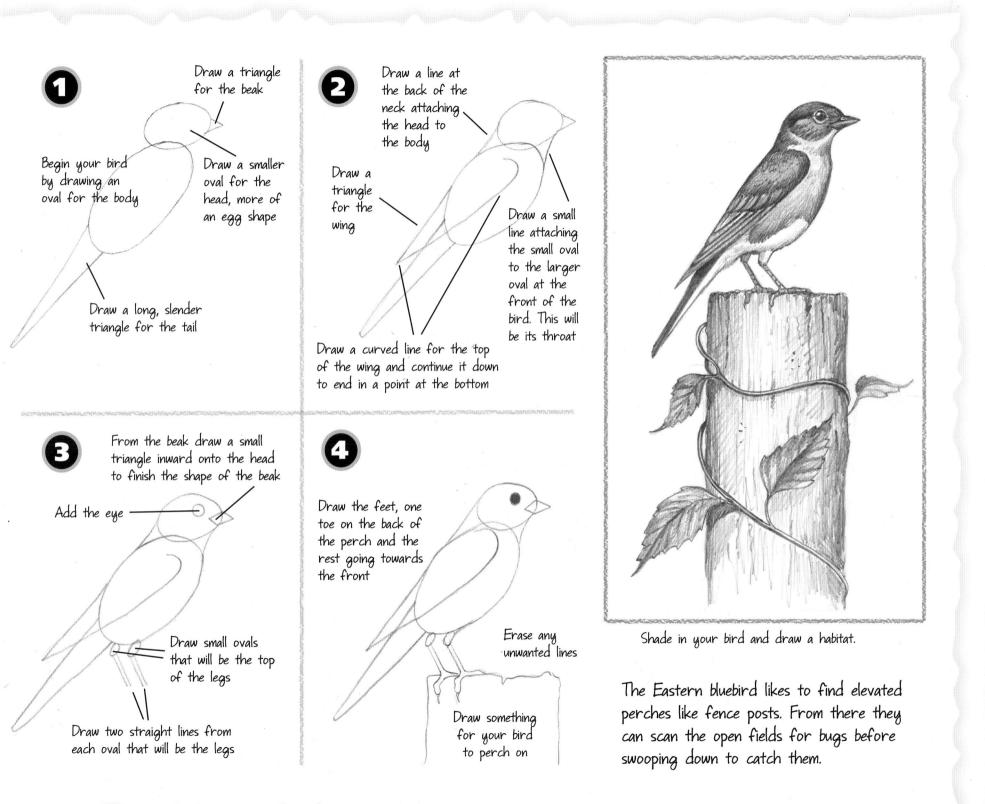

1

Draw a triangle for the beak

Begin your bird by drawing an oval for the body

Draw a smaller oval for the head, more of an egg shape

Draw a long, slender triangle for the tail

2

Draw a line at the back of the neck attaching the head to the body

Draw a triangle for the wing

Draw a small line attaching the small oval to the larger oval at the front of the bird. This will be its throat

Draw a curved line for the top of the wing and continue it down to end in a point at the bottom

3

From the beak draw a small triangle inward onto the head to finish the shape of the beak

Add the eye

Draw small ovals that will be the top of the legs

Draw two straight lines from each oval that will be the legs

4

Draw the feet, one toe on the back of the perch and the rest going towards the front

Erase any unwanted lines

Draw something for your bird to perch on

Shade in your bird and draw a habitat.

The Eastern bluebird likes to find elevated perches like fence posts. From there they can scan the open fields for bugs before swooping down to catch them.

Ducks

There are several different types of ducks within the large family of ducks. One type is the "diver ducks". They are called "diver ducks" because they use the method of diving underwater for their food, sometimes diving to a depth of almost 30 feet. They dive to eat vegetation, aquatic insects, fish eggs, snails, and minnows.

Some ducks are called "puddle ducks". This is because they tend to live in small ponds and lakes. They prefer to eat their food from the surface of the water. They feed on plants, seeds and duckweed on the top of the water rather than diving for their dinner. They will often use a technique called "dabbling" where they put their head and neck under the water and tip their bodies up so they can reach for food farther under the waters' surface.

1 Start softly with basic shapes—an oval, a circle and a small triangle for the beak

2 Draw the inside of the bill

Draw a small wing

Use lines to make a soft point at the end of your large oval which will be the tail

3 Add the eye

Start the legs with two small ovals

4 Draw legs

Add feet

Erase all your extra lines

Wood ducks make their nests up in the trees to avoid predators. When it comes time for the babies to leave the nest they have been known to just drop down from the branch where they will bounce on the ground.

Loons

Loons spend almost their entire lives in the water. A pair of loons will mate for life, returning to the same lake every year to make their nest. They build their nest together and there the female will lay 1-2 olive colored, speckled eggs. Less than a day after hatching, the babies will be swimming in the water. They climb on their parent's backs for protection and rest.

Loons are very territorial, often chasing other loons from their lake.

Loons usually place their nests near the edge of the water, preferably on an island on the lake, so they can avoid predators. They will often use the same nest as the year before. Their nests are built out of reeds, grass, mud and leaves.

The common loon is the second largest loon in the loon family. It can average about 30 inches in length and weigh an average of 10 pounds. Its wingspan can reach 5 feet. The males and females look very similar in appearance.

Loons primarily dine on fish but will also eat insects, frogs, crayfish and even leeches. They are expert divers and use their large, webbed feet, which are placed far back on their bodies, to propel themselves through the water and to dive deeply to catch their food.

1 Softly begin your drawing by making the general shape of the loon with basic shapes

Draw a triangle for the bill

Use an oval for the head

Draw a larger, long oval for the body

Use lightly drawn curved lines for the neck

Start softly connecting your basic shapes together to get the outline of the Loon

2 Place a curved line where the neck meets the oval of the body to attach the neck to the body

Add a triangle to the oval of the body for the tail

3 Add an eye

Add the lines that make the wing

Attach the bill to the head by drawing a small triangle on the inside of the head

At this point erase any unwanted lines

4 A loon has white spots on its body — draw them now

Add the white stripes that are on a loon's neck

Carefully shade around the stripes and darken in the head

Carefully shade around the white spots

At this point you can create a habitat for your loon

Turtles

There are more than 250 varieties of turtles and tortoises throughout the world. Some, like the Eastern box turtle, live only on land, seldom entering water more than 1–2 inches deep.

Other turtles, like the soft-shell turtle, live most of their lives in the water, coming out only to lay eggs and sun their shell occasionally.

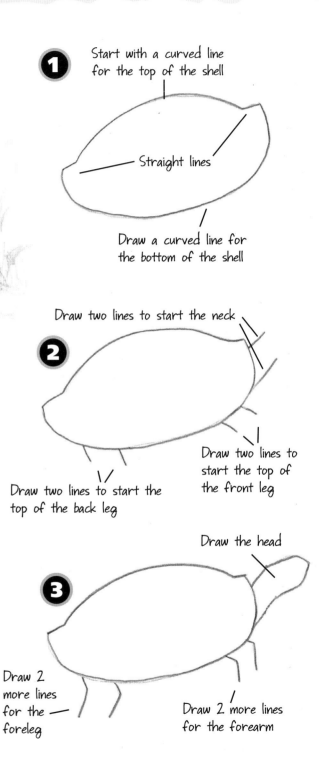

1 Start with a curved line for the top of the shell

Straight lines

Draw a curved line for the bottom of the shell

2 Draw two lines to start the neck

Draw two lines to start the top of the front leg

Draw two lines to start the top of the back leg

3 Draw the head

Draw 2 more lines for the foreleg

Draw 2 more lines for the forearm

4

Add the tail

Add a line to define the neck

Draw front foot

Draw back foot

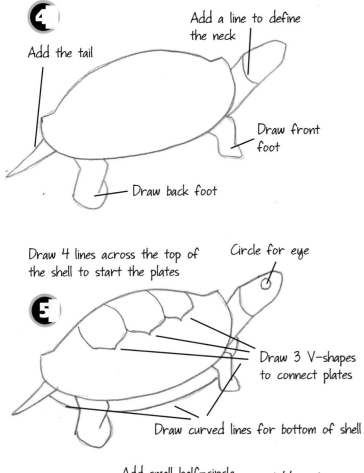

5

Draw 4 lines across the top of the shell to start the plates

Circle for eye

Draw 3 V-shapes to connect plates

Draw curved lines for bottom of shell

The painted turtle is one of the most colorful turtles, with red and yellow markings occurring on the shell and head. They can sometimes grow to a shell length of 10 inches.

6

Add small half-circle for other eye

Add pupil

Draw curved line to follow the shape of the shell

Draw many small squares around the edge of the shell

7

Connect top plates to bottom plates

Add toenails

8

Add spots to small plates

Add painted lines

Draw mouth

Add painted lines to legs & tail

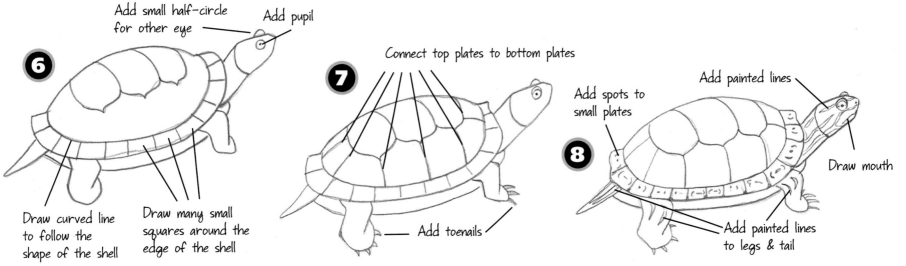

Herons

There are many different types of herons, from the great blue and little blue to the great white and the much smaller night heron.

The great blue heron is the largest of the American herons. It stands about four feet tall and has a wingspan of almost six feet.

Great blue herons are experts at sneaking up on their food. They will stand motionless in the shallow water and wait to catch fish, frogs, crawfish and insects with their long, sharp bills. When they catch something, they swallow it whole.

Herons hunt by themselves but nest in groups. These nesting colonies are called rookeries.

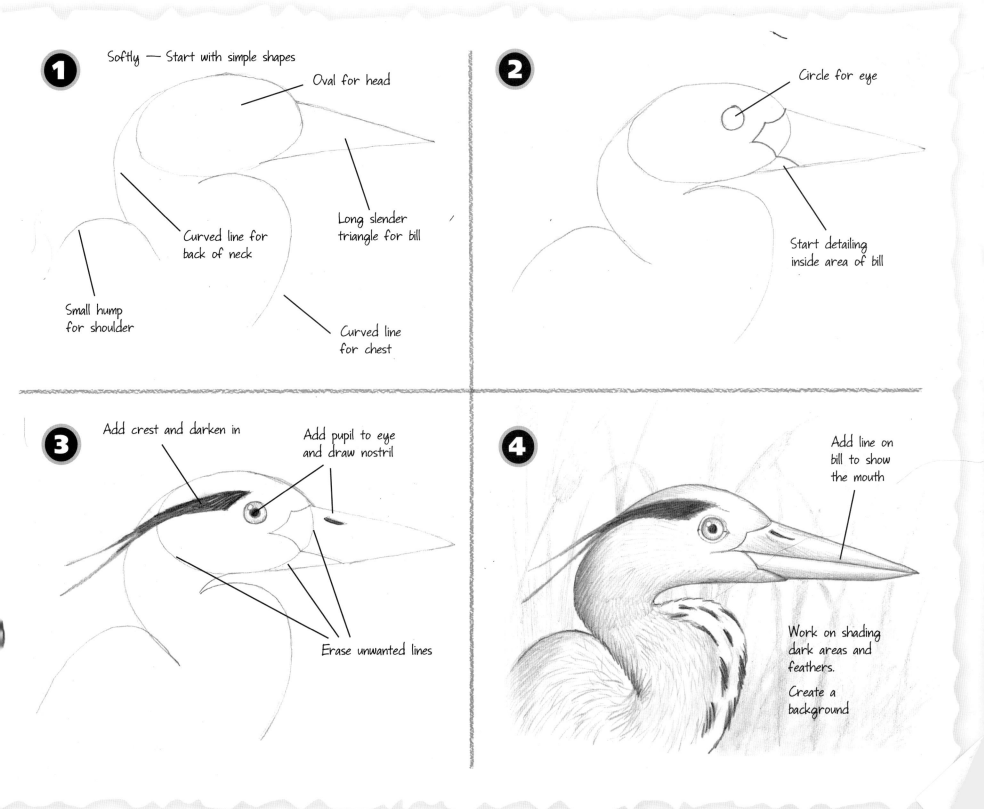

1 Softly — Start with simple shapes

Oval for head

Long slender triangle for bill

Curved line for back of neck

Small hump for shoulder

Curved line for chest

2 Circle for eye

Start detailing inside area of bill

3 Add crest and darken in

Add pupil to eye and draw nostril

Erase unwanted lines

4 Add line on bill to show the mouth

Work on shading dark areas and feathers.

Create a background

Frogs

There are thousands of different varieties of frogs and toads. Some, like treefrogs prefer to spend most of life living in trees. Other frogs, like the bullfrog, spend most of their lives in ponds, lakes and streams.

Treefrog

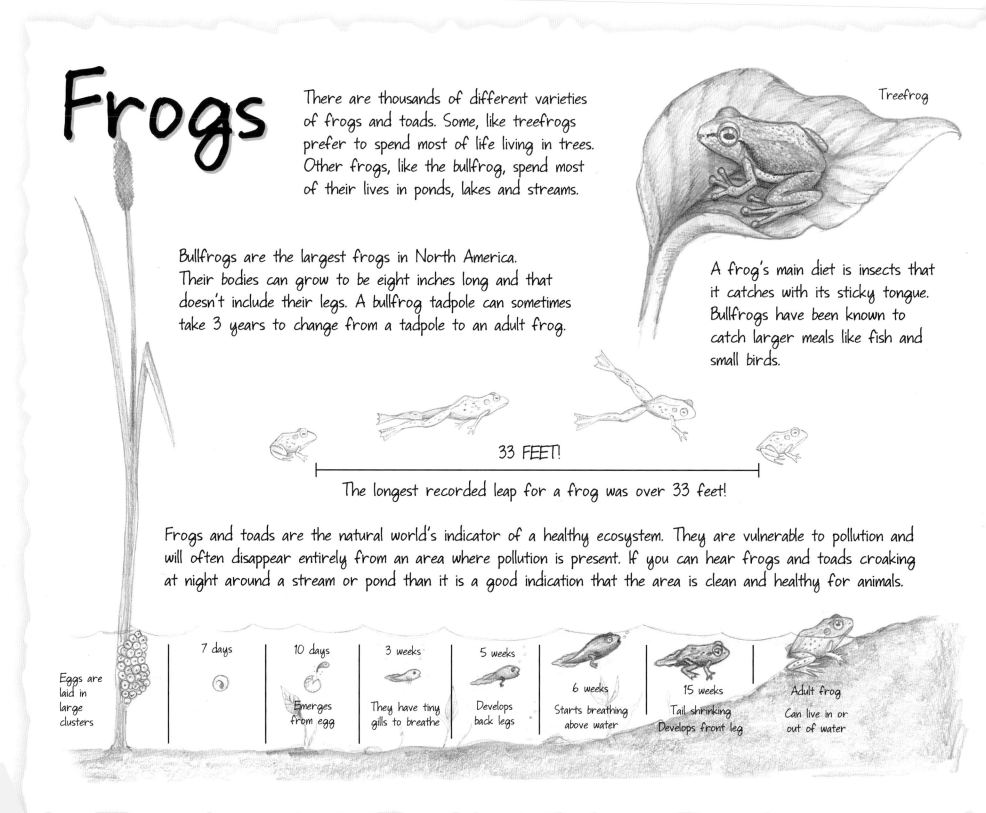

Bullfrogs are the largest frogs in North America. Their bodies can grow to be eight inches long and that doesn't include their legs. A bullfrog tadpole can sometimes take 3 years to change from a tadpole to an adult frog.

A frog's main diet is insects that it catches with its sticky tongue. Bullfrogs have been known to catch larger meals like fish and small birds.

33 FEET!

The longest recorded leap for a frog was over 33 feet!

Frogs and toads are the natural world's indicator of a healthy ecosystem. They are vulnerable to pollution and will often disappear entirely from an area where pollution is present. If you can hear frogs and toads croaking at night around a stream or pond than it is a good indication that the area is clean and healthy for animals.

Eggs are laid in large clusters

7 days

10 days
Emerges from egg

3 weeks
They have tiny gills to breathe

5 weeks
Develops back legs

6 weeks
Starts breathing above water

15 weeks
Tail shrinking
Develops front leg

Adult frog
Can live in or out of water

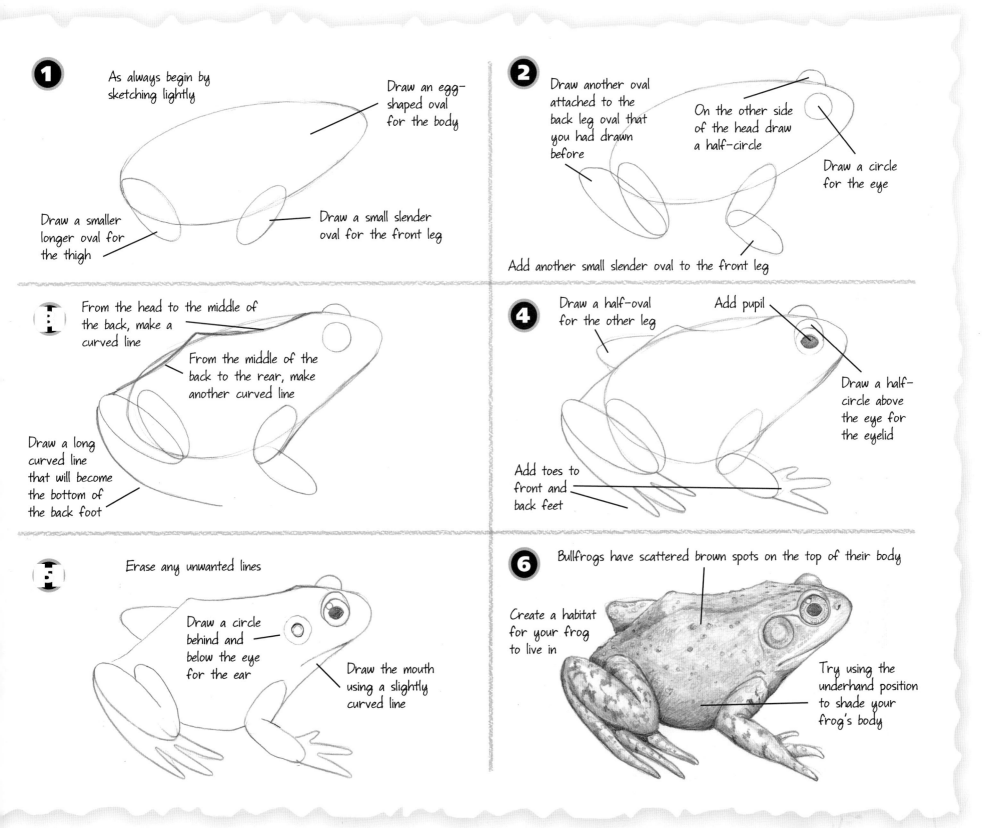

1 As always begin by sketching lightly

Draw an egg-shaped oval for the body

Draw a smaller longer oval for the thigh

Draw a small slender oval for the front leg

2 Draw another oval attached to the back leg oval that you had drawn before

On the other side of the head draw a half-circle

Draw a circle for the eye

Add another small slender oval to the front leg

3 From the head to the middle of the back, make a curved line

From the middle of the back to the rear, make another curved line

Draw a long curved line that will become the bottom of the back foot

4 Draw a half-oval for the other leg

Add pupil

Draw a half-circle above the eye for the eyelid

Add toes to front and back feet

5 Erase any unwanted lines

Draw a circle behind and below the eye for the ear

Draw the mouth using a slightly curved line

6 Bullfrogs have scattered brown spots on the top of their body

Create a habitat for your frog to live in

Try using the underhand position to shade your frog's body

Rabbits

The cottontail rabbit is found throughout most of North America. Even though it is a part of the rabbit family the female builds its nest much like a hare would. She will dig a small hole or depression in the ground that she will line with fur and grass. The babies are born furless and with their eyes closed. When the mother leaves to eat she will cover the defenseless babies with more fur and grass to hide them from view.

Rabbits and hares can be found almost anywhere in the world. There are several differences between rabbits and hares. One difference is that hares are larger than rabbits. They also have longer ears and legs. These longer legs allow hares to jump much higher than rabbits. The jack rabbits of the western states are actually hares.

jack rabbit

1

2 small, slender ovals to start ears

Draw an egg shape for the head

Start the body with a long oval

2

Add eye

Half-circle for hip

Small, curved line for front of leg

Angled line for back of front leg

3

V-shape for nose

Add foot

2 curved lines for other front leg

Long, slender oval for back foot

4

Shape ears by making them slightly pointed at the top

Add white eye patch

Add tail

Half-circle for cheek

Add foot

Erase unwanted lines

Add the other back foot

5

Create fur on the head & body by "crosshatching," a method which looks like many small x-shapes next to each other. This will take some time.

Erase unwanted lines

Outline the bunny with short, rough lines to make it look like fur

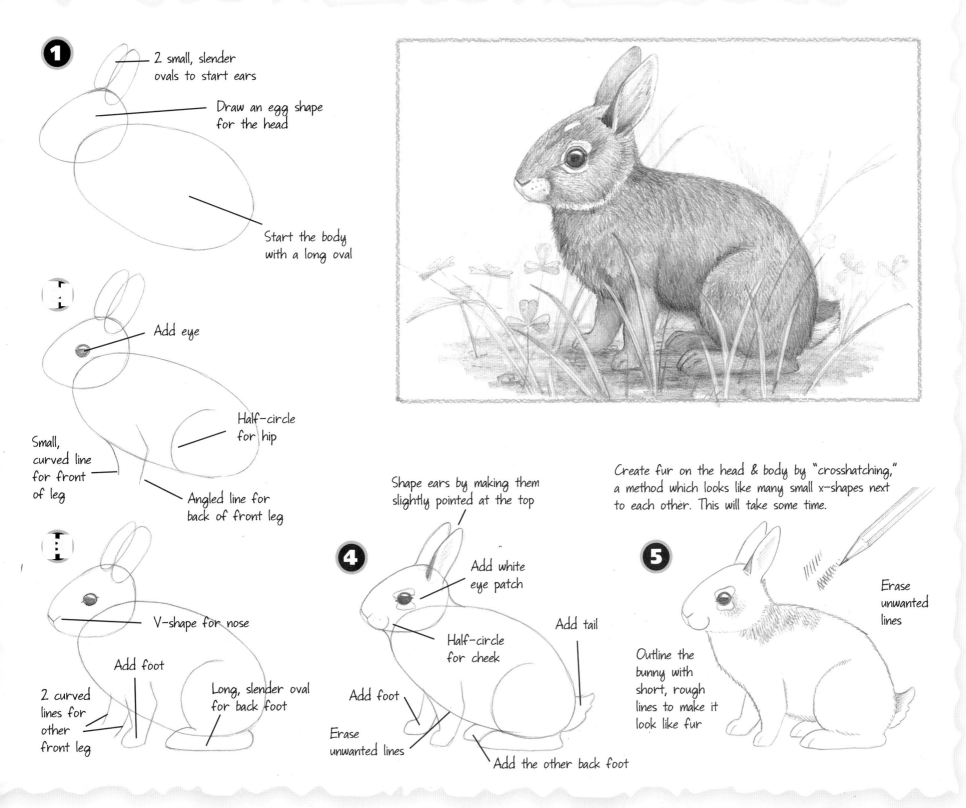

White-tailed Deer

Beginning in the late winter and early spring the male white-tailed deer will shed its old antlers, which means they fall off. New antlers will begin to grow almost immediately. The shed antlers provide a food source for small animals. They will devour them very quickly. That's why it is a very rare and lucky thing to find a dropped antler in the woods.

White-tailed deer are very good jumpers and have been known to jump fences that are 6 feet and higher to get to the food on the other side.

The white-tailed deer gets its name because of the white fur on the underside of its tail. As with most mammals the male, called the buck, is larger than the female, or doe.
The buck grows a set of antlers every year. When they are growing they will be covered in a soft fur called "velvet". When the antlers are done growing and have hardened, the buck will rub off the velvet using trees and shrubs. These rub spots, which the buck leaves behind on the trees, help to mark his territory.

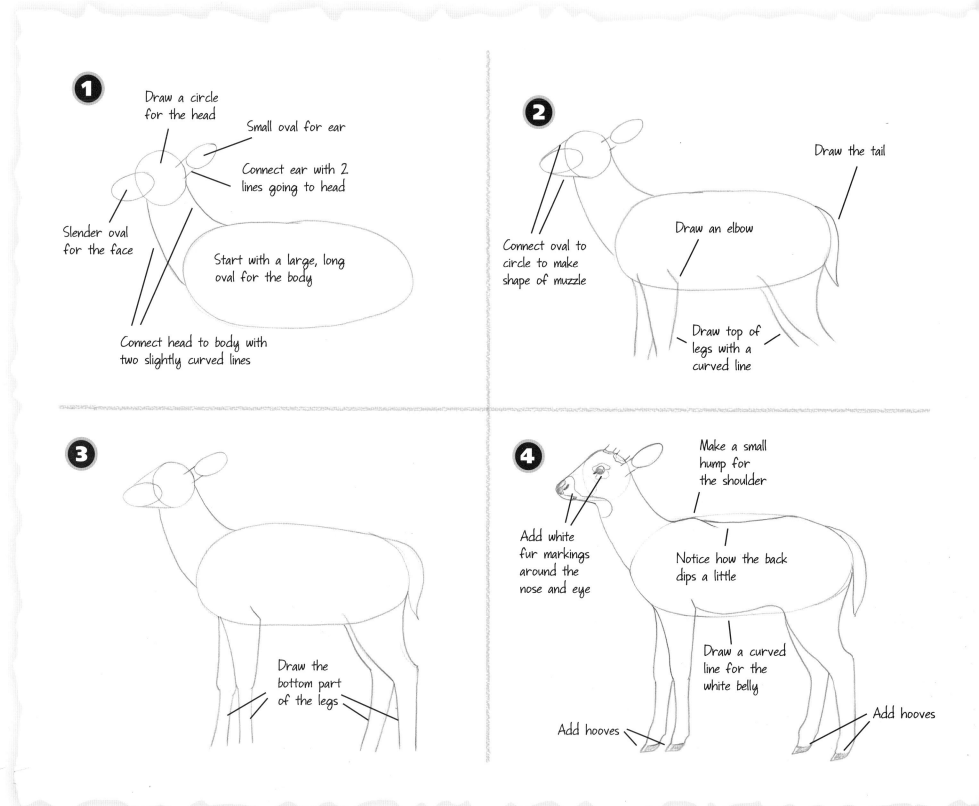

1

Draw a circle for the head

Small oval for ear

Connect ear with 2 lines going to head

Slender oval for the face

Start with a large, long oval for the body

Connect head to body with two slightly curved lines

2

Draw the tail

Draw an elbow

Connect oval to circle to make shape of muzzle

Draw top of legs with a curved line

3

Draw the bottom part of the legs

4

Make a small hump for the shoulder

Add white fur markings around the nose and eye

Notice how the back dips a little

Draw a curved line for the white belly

Add hooves

Add hooves

5

Start antlers

Notice that the antlers begin by growing backwards

Erase all unwanted lines

Antler Growth

6

Main beam

These are called "browtines", and they point up

Deer antlers can have many points, but most have 3-5 on each main beam & they grow up toward the sky

Notice that the antlers begin by growing backwards & then curve over the face

7

White-tailed deer are usually reddish-brown in color most of the year. In the winter, their fur changes to a grayish tone.

White-tailed Fawns

A healthy white-tailed doe can have one to two fawns each spring and can sometimes carry three. If a doe has more than one fawn she will hide them in different areas while she feeds.

Within twenty minutes of being born a fawn is able to stand for the first time and within three to four hours it is strong enough to follow its mother.

A fawn's colors and spots help camouflage them as they lay hidden on the forest floor.

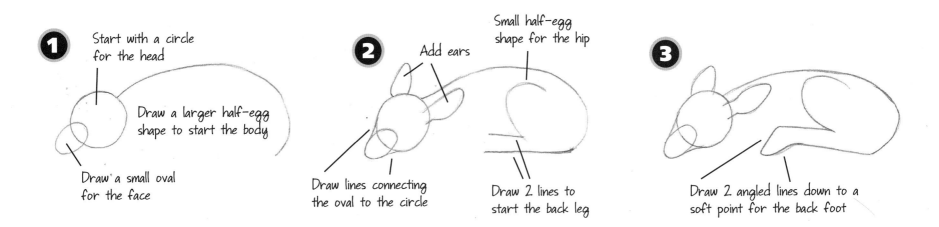

1 Start with a circle for the head

Draw a larger half-egg shape to start the body

Draw a small oval for the face

2 Add ears

Small half-egg shape for the hip

Draw lines connecting the oval to the circle

Draw 2 lines to start the back leg

3 Draw 2 angled lines down to a soft point for the back foot

4

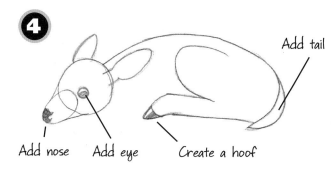

Add tail

Add nose   Add eye   Create a hoof

5

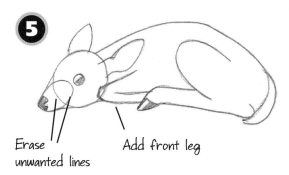

Erase unwanted lines

Add front leg

A fawn is born with no scent so predators can pass very close and never realize the fawn is there. Newborn fawns also instinctively know to freeze when they sense danger.

Many people find fawns in the woods and mistakenly believe they are abandoned. Actually, the mother has hidden them while she goes to find food.

6

Add white spots

Draw white areas around the nose and eye

7

Carefully shade the fawn's body around the white spots